The
POWER
Of
SURRENDER

Rev J Martin

DEDICATION

I dedicate this book to my dad who recently died. May he rest in peace

CONTENTS

ACKNOWLEDGMENTS

This book would not have been possible without the support and encouragement of my family, and the inspiration from my Heavenly Father.

A special thanks to: my editor; Pixal Design Studios for the design work, and Amazon for providing the digital tools by which I can get my message out into the world.

Finally, I would like to thank YOU, for buying my book, may it enlighten your life and bring you peace.

Introduction

In the same way that you can't force a flower to bloom or a seed to germinate, you can't force life to happen on your timetable, by your rules. You must trust in the process of life. You must learn to surrender to the will of God.

We all tend to want to control everything for our life to work out as we have planned. We want our destiny to happen in a specific order, and when it doesn't, it can lead to worry, doubt, and stress, which can lead to us feeling that we must do something because we cannot see another way.

When our plan doesn't work out, the best solution available is to pray for the highest good. When we pray, we become open to the fact that a disappointment or obstacle can be a detour to put us in the right direction.

It's important to remember that God's plan for us can take many detours. That his plan can take us places that we would never go on our own —resulting in us doing something more wonderful, more impactful, more meaningful, and helping more people than we had initially planned. However, most people get caught up in their negative thoughts. Instead of looking for the positives, they focus on what is not working, what is not going well, and that creates resistance. Worry, doubt, and fear are all part of this resistance, giving us the illusion of control.

So the question naturally arises, what do I do if I'm stuck in worry, doubt, and fear? In judgement, hurt, or anger?

What most of us do is we add another level of judgment on top of it. While we know that we shouldn't worry, doubt, or think the worst, we can't help it. So, we add to it. How did I let this happen? Why did I not see this coming? Why did I let them treat me in this way?

We tend to get caught up in our thoughts, overanalyzing events. So instead of focusing on everything that is going right, we focus on what is going wrong—creating a negative thought loop that is difficult to break.

When we surrender, we give up, but it's not the way that we think about giving up. We don't give up on the situation, we give up on the notion that we are in control; we give up on the overanalyzing, trusting that everything will work out as planned.

Gaining Trust

Many don't surrender because they don't trust that there is anything to take care of them, carry them, or show them the way. But when we finally let go of the reins, acknowledging our lack of control, something remarkable happens. We get the opportunity to directly experience being supported by a force more powerful than ourselves, what I like to call supernatural grace. Which once experienced can never be forgotten.

We never learn the power of surrender and its unlimited potential or that this power is at our disposal and can be used to work miracles in our lives.

Stop the overthinking today and raise your awareness to new heights.

Proverbs 3:5-6

Trust in the LORD with all your heart and lean not on your own understanding; in all your ways submit to him, and he will make your paths straight.

Faith Has Two Parts

A man started to walk on a tight rope 200ft above the city below. As he walked, he balanced himself using a long stick. As impressive as it was to the crowd, what was even more impressive was the second time he crossed his son was sitting on his shoulders. Everyone below watched, tense beyond words. Some were praying; others found it hard to look, half-expecting the man to fall.

As he reached the other side with his son, the crowd clapped, whistled, and cheered with utter delight. Praising him for his magnificent feat. Then he called down to everyone, "Do you think I can do it again?" The crowd shouted back in unison, "Yes, Yes, Yes, you can."

"Do you trust me." He asked. Again, they shouted, "Yes."

Then he asked the crowd, "Which one of you will sit on my shoulders this time? I will take you to the other side safely." Everyone fell silent. No one said anything; they just looked at him in shock. After a few minutes, people started to walk away.

Belief is very different from trust. The crowd believed the man could walk the tight rope, they had seen him do it twice before, once with his son on his shoulders, but they didn't trust him to bring them across safely.

For trust, you need total surrender. It's this trust that is lacking towards God in our world today. All Christians believe they have the utmost faith, but few trust him with their lives. Few trust that everything will work out as planned.

Psalm 20:7
"Some trust in chariots and some in horses, but we trust in the name of the LORD our God."

Gods Rosebud

A man went to see his minister, feeling insecure about how a certain situation would turn out. He had done all that he could but couldn't stop worrying.

The minister sat and listened to all that his visitor had to say. When the man had finished, the minister got up and asked the visitor to take a walk with him in his garden.

They walked in silence, then the minister walked up to a rosebush and handed the man a rosebud and told him to open it without tearing off any of the petals.

The man looked in disbelief at the minister. He was trying to figure out what a rosebud could have to do with his problem. But because of his great respect for the older man, he proceeded to try to unfold the rose, while keeping every petal intact. It wasn't long before the man realized it was impossible.

Noticing the man's inability to unfold the rosebud
without tearing it, the minister began to recite the
following poem:

It is only a tiny rosebud,
a flower of God's design;
But I cannot unfold the petals
with these clumsy hands of mine.

The secret of unfolding flowers
is not known to such as I.
God opens this flower so easily,
but in my hands, they die.

If I cannot unfold a rosebud,
this flower of God's design,
then how can I have the wisdom
to unfold this life of mine?

So, I'll trust in God for leading
each moment of my day.
I will look to God for guidance,
in each step along the way.

The path that lies before me,
only my Lord and Saviour knows.
I'll trust God to unfold the moments,
just as He unfolds the rose.

Author unknown.

Whatever you may currently be unfolding in your life, please do your best not to worry, knowing that it will turn out all right. We like to think that stressing over a problem will somehow help, but this is very rarely the case.

When you are in self-will, God leaves you to it, but the moment that you surrender—his grace begins to flow. And peace will take the place of any fear that you may feel.

Proverbs 23:26
My son give me your heart and let your eyes delight in my ways.

Thy Will Be Done

Roman 12:2

Do not conform to the pattern of this world but be transformed by the renewing of your mind. Then you will be able to test and approve what God's will is—his good, pleasing and perfect will.

One of the reasons we shouldn't focus on the past is that it's out of our control. Yet, so many of us let past experiences spill over into the present.

There is no benefit from focusing on the past, but we do so naturally. However, if we allow our past mistakes to determine our decisions in the present, we can become more fearful, more stressed, and more depressed.

Similarly, if you worry about the future, you cast your fears into the future. You doubt that your future self will be any better, which is detrimental to your confidence. When you doubt, worry, or stress over a situation, then you're not in a state of surrender. You are assuming that you know the future. You are assuming your future will be the same as your past. You are assuming you know more than God—that your will over the situation is more superior.

If for example, you have an interview coming up, and you pray, but then you go over every little thing that could go wrong, then more than likely the interview will not go well. But if you renew your mind to the truth that "if getting the job is in your destiny—you will get it," then with that act of surrender comes calmness and peace.

The negative thoughts will come, but it's up to you to make good decisions when they do. Whether you have a good or bad future is dependent on the choices you make. You can choose fear, or you can choose to have faith.

Each choice of faith is renewing your mind to the fact that there is a higher power in control.

Ephesians 4:22-24

You were taught, with regard to your former way of life, to put off your old self, which is being corrupted by its deceitful desires; to be made new in the attitude of your minds; and to put on the new self, created to be like God in true righteousness and holiness.

From today forward you can decide to renew your mind. You can decide to worry less. You can decide to be less doubtful; you can decide to surrender to the will of God. You can be less stressed, less tense, and more relaxed.

If you make it a daily routine to surrender, then your mind will renew, and your life will change. You can't change the past, and the only way that you can change the future is by the decisions you make in the present. And you do that by throwing out the thoughts of worry, doubt, and fear. Thinking instead thoughts of faith, peace, love, joy, and happiness.

Begin to renew your mind and surrender to the will of God.

Renewal Prayer

Divine Intelligence created my body and all its organs. This Divine Intelligence beats my heart over 100,000 times a day. It is responsible for trillions of chemical reactions necessary to keep me alive. So, I surrender to God in part; now it's time to surrender to God in full.

Live and Learn From Great Loss

A good friend had a troublesome relationship with his dad. Michael (name changed for confidentiality) did the best he could, but it was never enough.

When his brothers turned eighteen, they limited their contact, but my friend, no matter how much he was hurt, went back for more. He kept working at the relationship, hoping one day it would improve.

Michael's dad died last year. Everyone expected him to get over his dad's death quickly, even Michael, as the dark force that had belittled him for so long was no longer there. The first year he found hard, but now into the second year, he was finding it even worse, which he didn't understand.

He told me he was having trouble sleeping, and his health was not the best. No doctor knew what was going on. Michael didn't understand why he couldn't just move on with his life. Now with the freedom to do what he wanted, he felt like something was holding him back.

From listening to my friend, it was clear he had not dealt with his father's death. He was trying to push his feelings to one side, thinking that because his relationship was destructive, he could get over the loss quickly. He went on to tell me he had been to see a counselor, revealing that, on one occasion, he broke down and the anger that surfaced scared him.

My friend didn't understand the anger, but I did. Every time that Michael's dad had hurt him, he had suppressed the anger rather than let it out. He suppressed the feelings for so long he didn't know they were there.

When we try to avoid grief, due to hurt or anger, the negative feelings will remain within—affecting our mental and physical health like in Michael's case. No matter your relationship with a parent, they brought you into the world, and they did the best they could. Being a parent is one of the hardest jobs, and sadly very few people are up to the challenge.

When I asked him if he had any unforgiveness towards his dad, he said no. But suppressed anger is a form of unforgiveness. Michael bottled the anger up inside, rather than get angry with his dad for hurting him. The suppressed feelings needed to be released.

For Michael to heal, he needed to forgive his dad for years of hurt. Forgiveness is the ultimate form of surrender. You are giving up the feelings of hurt, pain, and anger to God so that you can move on with your life. A good analogy for unforgiveness—if you tied a small weight onto your leg every time you got hurt or offended. The burden would build up until one day you would find it hard to move around.

In the same way that you would find it difficult to walk with weights on your legs, you will find it difficult to walk into situations similar to the ones that caused you to hurt in the past.

For example, if you got hurt in a relationship and never forgave that person for the hurt, then you may go into every relationship with the same pain. Meaning, you have your guard up, almost expecting to be hurt again.

A lot of people, like Michael, carry around the heavyweight of unforgiveness for so long they forget that it's there. The unforgiveness has become part of them, affecting every area of their lives.

To release the suppressed anger, I advised Michael to write out what was troubling him in as much detail as possible. All the hurts from the past, everything he wanted to say to his father but couldn't—holding nothing back. Starting each sentence with I forgive. Getting all the feelings out on paper releases the negative emotions within.

The next step was to go outside and burn it, watching the negative energy evaporate into smoke. A deep hurt can be triggered easily, so I advised Michael to repeat the process as often as necessary. After a couple of times, the negative feelings would subside and not have the same control over him. Until one day all the negative energy would be gone.

When we suppress hurt from the past, it can affect our mental and physical health. Surrendering to the will of God, passing all our troubles over to Him allows us to experience the fullness of life.

Most Powerful Healer

If we hold a grudge, for example, we may feel in control. We may feel we have something over the other person because they owe us something. The opposite is true. When we don't forgive, the anger, resentment, or grievance has control over us.

Forgiveness allows us to regain control of our emotions, our feelings, and our lives. Which means we no longer let certain people or circumstances affect us. Forgiveness doesn't happen instantly; it is a process of surrender and re-surrender. It requires you to continue to choose forgiveness whenever the negative feelings resurface—old thoughts mean you are healing not that you haven't forgiven the person.

Many think that to forgive means that you are weak, which is far from the truth. When you forgive, it shows strength, reflecting courage and wisdom. Gandhi, a famous spiritual teacher, once said, "the weak can never forgive. Forgiveness is an attribute of the strong."

Another misconception is that if you forgive someone that the relationship is back on track. Not the case. If someone hurt you or broke your trust, it would be unhealthy for you to let that person back into your life, as you could open yourself up to more potential pain.

Many people get confused about what forgiveness means, and that's what stops them from doing it. Forgiveness does not mean that you must let the other person know. It is between you and God, so your conscience is clear. Forgiveness is a very selfish act for you and you alone. When we can practice forgiveness, our physical health improves, our mental health improves, and our spiritual life flourishes.

When Michael did the necessary work to release his anger, his health and sleep got better. Now he has his own company. Michael is giving motivational talks at youth centers all across Europe. The central part of his story is that he turned his feelings about his relationship with his dad into the fuel to propel him to the next level of his destiny.

When we hold onto the past, we cannot embrace the future.

Better Future Than Your Past

Many people can't forget what happened in the past. Maybe they were hurt. Perhaps they made a mistake, or maybe they didn't get a good start in life. Events can affect your confidence and self-worth.

By holding onto the past, you're not allowing your destiny to unfold. A good analogy is driving to work while looking in your rear-view mirror.

Now, you may think that is crazy, and you are right it is crazy, but that is what people are doing every day. They let past hurts, disappointments, and regrets make them depressed and anxious in the present. Their life can't go anywhere because they are looking back, letting their past dictate their future.

Some people lose a loved one to illness and never get over the pain. Others lose a loved one to illness and set up a charity—helping to give support to families in a similar situation. They turn their pain of loss into love.

We all want our lives to work out the way we have planned. But when they don't, we can get frustrated. The disappointment can lead to stubbornness, leading to us forcing our will on a situation. Only for it to get worse. When my plans don't work out, what I like to do is to take a step back—never making a decision when I'm frustrated or angry. Emotions cloud our vision, and more often than not lead to us making the wrong decision.

It took me many years to surrender to God's will for my life. For years I couldn't see how setbacks could turn in my favor—leading to stress, worry, and fear. However, the wiser I grew, the more I realized God's ways were not my ways.

It's human nature to want to go from A to B. It's not logical for A to go to P then to B, but this is the way that God likes to work. We're taken on detours to learn lessons. However, if you try to go to B when life wants to go to P, it will lead to worry, doubt, and anger: even depression and ill-health.

If your life doesn't seem to work out, no matter how hard you pray, then the best solution is to surrender to the will of God. Take a step back and look at the bigger picture.

Maybe you keep getting turned down for a promotion because it is a sign that you need to change careers. Maybe you have outgrown the group of friends that has started to talk behind your back. Maybe your hard childhood was to teach you how not to raise your children.

God closes doors and puts us through situations for a reason. Many times, it doesn't make sense, but it always works out for the greater good. God can see what we cannot. Don't question everything that goes against you, often a setback or hurt is for your protection from something greater.

One of the main lessons I have learned is not to knock on a door that God has closed—questioning why certain events happened the way they did. Too many people refuse to accept God's will and as a result, add a lot of unnecessary pressure on themselves.

If you find yourself trying to force something to happen, then it's often a sign that you need to surrender and let your divine destiny flow with ease and grace.

How to Get Over A Betrayal?

A successful businessman who was married with three children had built his company from scratch. One day, his business partner wasn't in the office, and when he got home that night, his wife was gone—leaving the children behind. He later learned that his wife and partner had been conspiring together. To strip the business of its assets, then go off together. Now they were gone.

His wife and partner had moved to another country, and the legal cost of going after them was more than he could afford. So, he turned all his attention to keep himself from going into personal bankruptcy.

His relationship with his children suffered as he became more and more preoccupied with how badly, how unfairly, how unjustly his wife had treated him. In final desperation, he turned to his minister for help.

His minister understood why he was angry and bitter—advising him that the only way to overcome the hurt was to surrender. To let go of the past.

Letting him know that if he did not, the anger and bitterness would consume him, affecting his mental health and his relationship with his children. Children who needed him now more than ever.

The man agreed with his minister but had no idea how he could surrender to that level of betrayal. So, the minister suggested to sitting down and writing a letter to his wife. Forgiving her for everything—wishing her well for the future. Only then could he move forward. Forgiveness was a step too far, so he left unhappy. Weeks went by, and his life got worse. Finally, he decided to write the letter and post it.

Later, he returned to his minister to thank him for his advice. Telling him that from the moment he posted the letter, he felt better, and his life started to improve. He sold his remaining assets and started a consulting company. Now he could work from home most days, which meant spending more time with his children than he ever had.

He could have easily let the hurt and betrayal get to him. Letting those feelings fester until they turned into anger, bitterness, and resentment, maybe resulting in him taking out his frustration on his children. Instead, he took his minister's advice, resulting in his relationship with his children becoming stronger.

When bad things happen, it's hard to move forward, but when you do, you will come into a new chapter of your life. When you forgive a hurt or betrayal, like this man did, you release the power that person has over you.

Remember, forgiveness is not condoning their behavior; it is detaching from it. Most of the people that hurt us want to see us upset; they want us to hold bitterness and resentment against them. That way, they can continue to hurt us for years to come.

You can claim back your power today by forgiving anyone that has hurt you in the past.

2 Timothy 4:18
"The Lord will rescue me from every evil deed and bring me safely into his heavenly kingdom."

Key Lesson From Abraham

In Genesis 22, God's command to Abraham to sacrifice his son, Isaac, is one of the most moving stories in the Bible. To test his faith and obedience, God commands Abraham to kill his only son as a burnt offering.

Without question, Abraham got up early the next morning, chopped wood for a fire, and saddled his donkey. Then he set off with his son Isaac to a mountain in the region of Moriah.

Not until Abraham had set the fire and tied his son to the altar did an angel appear to tell him not to hurt the lad in any way. Abraham's obedient surrender is the highest point of faith in all history. It's a level that we all aspire to have.

The Bible gives us direct commandments on how to live, telling us not to worry, not to fear. Instead, reminding us to be made new in the attitude of our minds. So, if your plan doesn't work out, don't get lost in negativity. Do like Abraham. Live with faith and obedience, and you will, like him, receive incredible blessings.

When Abraham was told to kill his only son, he could have questioned God's decision—spending time in pity and bitterness. Although, if he had, Abraham would never have been graced with countless descendants. Similarly, if we question God's path for our lives, by choosing to live in doubt, worry, or fear, then we too will never receive our blessings.

When you go through situations that you don't understand, it's not the end. It's often a test to see if you're ready to transcend to the next level of your destiny. If you can surrender like Abraham, God will deliver you something in return for the trust that you place in Him.

If you let yourself get caught up in the past or worry about the future, you can lose your way. Don't let one mistake define who you are. Don't let one experience, thought, or action determine your destiny. A lot of our worries, doubts, and fears will subside when we renew our minds with new thinking.

It's so easy to focus on what we cannot change. You cannot change the past. You cannot change another person's thoughts or actions. And you cannot change a person that doesn't want to change. So, don't waste your time trying.

Instead, focus your attention on the only thing you can change—how you react to negative thoughts and feelings.

Negative thoughts and feelings are not going to disappear, but when they do arise, you can choose to surrender and let them go. So, rather than giving your emotional energy to the people that hurt you, invest that energy into the people you love. Invest that energy into the people that believe in you—the people that support you in your time of need.

Abraham knew that if he kept his mind on what God wanted that his life would work out for the greater good. He could have attached to earthly things, feelings of pity or bitterness, but he knew better.

Colossians 3:2
Set your minds on things above, not on earthly things.

When we go through problems, we don't understand we need to keep our minds on the glory of God. "Your will be done, on earth as it is in heaven" (Matthew 6:10).

When you surrender and stop allowing negative feelings like anger, fear, and bitterness to dominate your thought life, then you enable the creator of the universe to come into your life and do what can sometimes seem like miracles. Too many people get caught up trying to control everything and miss out on so many wonderful experiences.

Ephesians 4:31
Get rid of all bitterness, rage and anger, brawling and slander, along with every form of malice. Be kind and compassionate to one another, forgiving each other, just as in Christ God forgave you.

What's Your Peace of Mind Worth?

Recently I got into a conversation with a young woman who had lost her job—an executive position she had held for several years. She had been to her lawyer and was going to sue for wrongful termination. She was both bitter and determined to get justice.

I asked her how long the process would take. She said it could take up to two years to get to court. Then I asked her what her chances were of winning her case. According to her lawyer, her chances were better than 50 percent.

Then I asked what she would do for the two years? She went on to tell me that if she took another position, it would weaken her case for compensation. If she pursued legal action, she would be tied up professionally and emotionally for up to two years. Then at the end of that time, there was a high chance she would lose her case in court. Ending up having gained nothing. She would have lost two years of her life preoccupied with her lawsuit. Not to mention the expenses involved. What advice would you give her? What would you do if someone mistreated you?

I suggested that she surrender, that she dropped the whole matter, that her happiness and peace of mind were far too important to be held at ransom for two years. No payoff or settlement was worth trading all that time.

She was both smart and perceptive, saying that she would give my advice some thought. Later I heard the young woman had dropped the legal action. Shortly afterwards, I read in the paper that she had taken a senior position with another company.

When something negative happens, it's good to take a step back and look at the bigger picture. Like in this woman's case, reflection on what enforcing her will on the situation would involve—two years of stress and uncertainty.

Life lesson: Setbacks can cause a lot of worry, doubt, and fear, but setbacks can be a signal to change direction or to change your approach.

No Surrender

My dad was a very religious man, but he had no patience. If something didn't work out the way he planned, then he would force his will on the situation. When old enough to offer my opinion, I would advise him to take a step back, but like most parents, he didn't listen to me. What did I know? I was only a child in his eyes.

From the sidelines, I had to watch my dad get further stressed when all his effort seemed to go in vain. I wasn't wise enough to know it then, but what my dad was doing was enforcing his will on the problem or difficulty. Rather than relaxing and taking a step back, he would go full steam ahead. If something was not to his liking, he wouldn't stop until he was happy with the outcome. Sometimes he won the battles but very often he didn't.

On one occasion, a neighbor cut a tree on the boundary line between the two properties. The neighbor was entirely in the wrong, but they were known for causing trouble in the community. They had an excellent lawyer and always won their case.

When my dad explained to me what had happened, I advised him to walk away, not to take the matter further. He said that he would, but as usual, went on ahead and did what he wanted to do. One solicitor letter turned into a court case which my dad sadly lost. In his angry state, he had said and done some things that strengthened their case.

Now, as you can imagine, he was furious. Again, I advised my dad to surrender, to let it go, and to let God be their judge. But my dad couldn't let it go. The neighbors kept annoying him, and each time they did, he took the bait. Within a couple of years, it led to another court case, which my dad lost again.

We later moved away, but my dad couldn't forget the injustice. Not long before he died, he made it clear never to have anything to do with our old neighbors. He had never forgiven them for what they put him through. The feelings of bitterness and resentment were as raw as ever. He took a hurt to his grave not because of what they did to him, but because he didn't listen to wise advice—to surrender the injustice to God.

When a situation is not working out for us, it's easy to feel like we must force our will. And yes, there are times when we must persist. But if you are coming from a place of fear, anger or hurt, it is often better to take a step back and listen to the advice of others.

The greatest lesson I learned from my dad was the lesson of surrender. If people want to hurt you deliberately, then don't meet negativity with negativity. Don't allow another person to affect your spirit.

Many people, like my old neighbors, are not connected to spirit, meaning they are unhappy most of the time. You might not think you have much, but when you have great faith and love, you radiate something that money can't buy. Some people will resent you for that quality; they will do whatever they can to drag you down. Please don't take their bait. Don't let them get you angry or upset. Don't play their games. Remain calm and pray for them. Soon they will move on to annoy someone else.

Your Spiritual Awakening

Once I read about a man called Jeff. Jeff had a condition that meant doctors had to remove one of his legs to save his life. He woke up from surgery an angry man. Now without a limb, he believed that his life was over. He blamed the doctors, he blamed himself, he even blamed God—he felt like his life was not worth living, resulting in him falling into depression. He began to use drugs and started drinking, which further deepened his negative state. Before long, he found himself referred to a therapist.

On their first meeting, she asked him to draw a picture of his body. He drew a picture of a vase with a huge jagged crack in it. She took his drawing and put in her desk drawer. Soon he started to ask how other young people coped with amputations. Later, he began to volunteer at a hospital with other young amputees like himself.

One day, he met a 21-year-old woman who was recovering from a double mastectomy and had a horrible history with breast cancer. He noticed that she never looked up from her hospital bed. After a few weeks of trying to get her attention, he looked down at his leg, took off his prosthetic device and dropped it and began to hop around.

Within a few minutes, she started laughing, and she looked up with a smile saying, "If you can dance, maybe I can sing."

Jeff went from angry, not seeing a way out of his situation, to accepting his fate. Asking, how can I help other people? Resulting in him pulling a broken young woman out of her depression. In the story, they later married.

In his last meeting with his therapist, she pulled out the drawing of the cracked vase, the picture he drew two years prior. She then asked him to illustrate how he felt now. He took the picture and said, "I need to finish this one."

Taking a yellow highlighter from her desk, he drew vibrant yellow lines coming out of the cracks in the vase. She looked at him, confused. Then he smiled and said, "the crack is what allowed my light to come through."

The cracks, the imperfections, the feelings of failure are where the light can shine through. When we get stuck, when something terrible happens, we need to surrender to the idea that it's a bad thing. We need to remember that "the setback, disappointment, or failure" is where the light can come through.

Matthew 5:16
In the same way, let your light shine before others, that they may see your good deeds and glorify your Father in heaven.

Let the Light Shine In

We are continually trying to have things go our way. From morning to night, we try to manage life so that it works out for us. Observe how constant it is. Even a small pause in this controlling opens up space for God's love to shine through.

We can bring this desire for control into every area of our lives. Only when we become aware of it, or when someone brings it to our attention will we even notice.

We judge ourselves and others all the time. Rarely thinking we are good enough. "If only certain situations would work out. Then I would be happy." The habit of controlling reduces the light that can flow into our lives. Controlling restricts the natural flow of life.

The more we've been hurt in the past, the more tightly we feel that we must manage everything. "I was hurt once it will never happen again." The need for certainty can bind us, reducing the infinite solutions available.

So how do we pause the controlling? And when I say pause, that doesn't mean to be inactive. We need to learn when to stop controlling so much. There is a time for action and a time for inaction. There is a time for everything and a season for every activity under the heavens (Ecclesiastes 3:1).

We need to learn to let go of the thoughts that we know don't help us, the feelings of worry, doubt, and fear. We know they make us more uptight, more stressed, and more depressed. More anxious about what could go wrong.

It was not until Jeff let go of the feelings of blame and anger, surrendering to God's will, that his life began to blossom.

An Exercise in Surrender

Scan the last week for a situation where you are aware of controlling whether it was trying to avoid judgement, trying to impress others, or trying to change a person's behavior. Some way that you were controlling concerning another person.

Look a little more closely at a situation where you had an agenda, where you were trying to get another person to respond in a certain way. Whether it was a family member, a friend, or somebody at work.

In this situation, how present were you? How open-hearted? How loving?

When you try to control someone, that person becomes an object that you, in some way, want to change. Surrendering the need to control is a way of reconnecting with our true nature.

Most humans have lost their connection to spirit. They have become confined to the material body. Their negative habits keep them stuck in a limited sense of who they are.

To reach the next level of your destiny, you will have to step outside your comfort zone. You will have to stop allowing your thoughts to pull you away from spirit and begin to renew your mind.

Please don't bring feelings of hurt, regret, or anger into a new year. Leave the negativity in the past; it doesn't belong in your future. You can't go through life holding onto hurts, bitterness, and wrong attitudes. Negativity will keep you from reaching new levels.

It's time to stop letting the failures of the past dictate your future; it's time to stop dwelling on hurts and disappointments. It's time to stop allowing fear to extinguish your faith. And it's time to start surrendering control, which will reveal the infinite possibilities available to you. Change your belief to trust. Everything will work out as God has planned.

If you do this, I believe and declare you are about to come into a spiritual awakening. New doors will open, new relationships will arise; you will experience favor, healing, breakthroughs, and the fullness of your destiny.

Feel the power of surrender; let God take control.

ABOUT THE AUTHOR

I live on the northwest coast of Ireland. I use this medium to share my true voice. I wish to enlighten others and help them to see that God wants the very best for them. We often make it hard for him to enter our lives as we focus on the dark clouds rather than the silver lining.

In this growing digital frontier I just want to shed a little light out into the world to light up peoples lives in the hope that they to will help inspire others which will slowly but surely change the world, even in a small way.

My Other Books

God's Perfect Timing
The Power Of Letting Go
The Power Of Choice
The Power Of Words
Make Space for God

Printed in Great Britain
by Amazon